José Letria is a well-known author in Portugal and has written many children's books including fiction and poetry. He has worked together with his son André on a number of picture books.

André Letria has been working as an illustrator since 1992 and was awarded the Portuguese illustration prize in the year 2000.

Maurice Riordan has published two collections of Poetry: *A Word from the Loki* and *Floods*.

For Rodrigo who has just arrived.

WingedChariot
Press

Supported by

  CALOUSTE GULBENKIAN FOUNDATION MINISTÉRIO DA CULTURA

The Moon Has Written You a Poem

Poems to read with children on moonlit nights

José Jorge Letria | André Letria

Translated and adapted by Maurice Riordan

WingedChariot Press

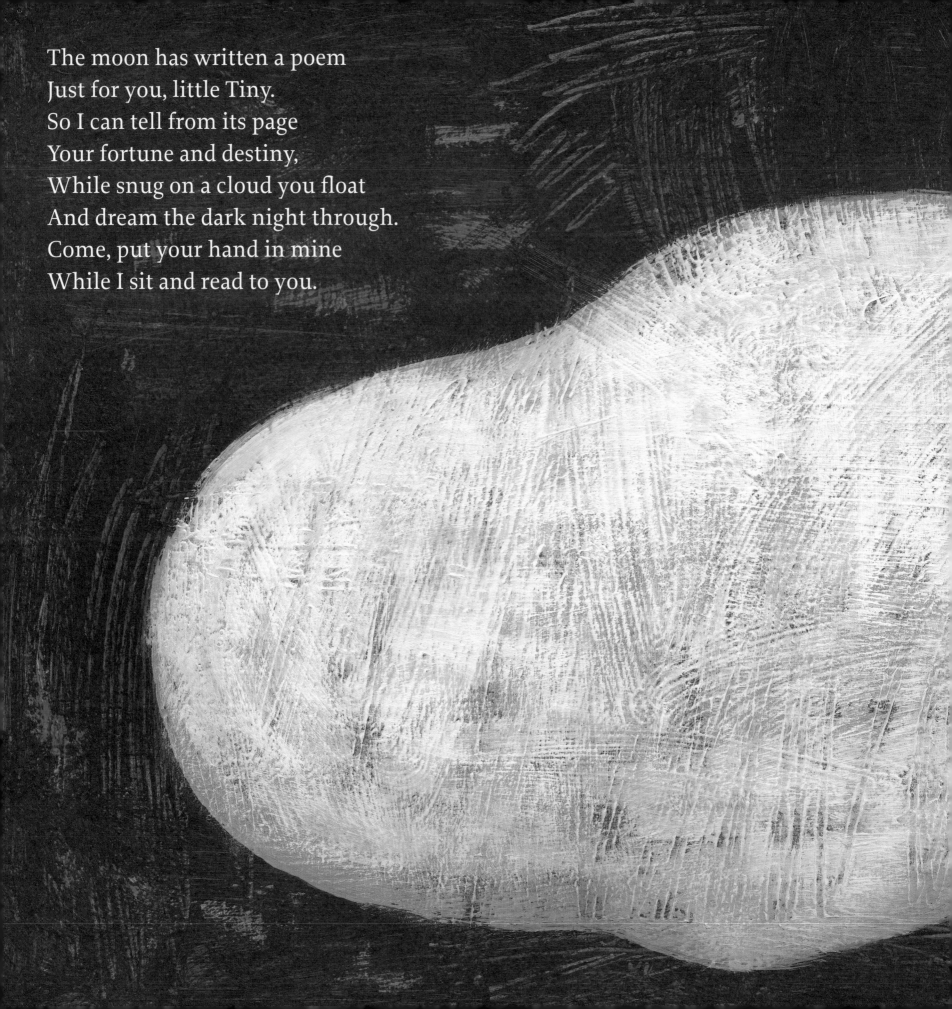

The moon has written a poem
Just for you, little Tiny.
So I can tell from its page
Your fortune and destiny,
While snug on a cloud you float
And dream the dark night through.
Come, put your hand in mine
While I sit and read to you.

The night has written a verse,
So I'll swing you in its cradle
Of Autumn's noisy winds.
Hush a bye, my baby!
Out come fairies and goblins,
Wicked elves and vampires
In cloaks from the misty fens
To dance around the bonfires.

The ocean has written a verse,
So this is what I'll do.
I'll learn to paint your smile
Because love asks me to,
Love that soars to heaven
On a seagull's outstretched wing,
With all its feathers trembling
As throats tremble when we sing.

Dreams have written a verse,
So I'll make for you this dream:
You're a dolphin, then an eel,
Now a salmon in the stream.
And as you read each line
It takes you in its clutches,
Since words can make a picture,
Like when an artist sketches.

And every word you read
Will name another part
Of the world's great forest
With its dark entangled heart.
But you'll learn its nooks and crannies,
When you begin to talk
And raid its flocks of sounds
As expert as a hawk.

And every word you say,
And some you can't pronounce,
Enchants you with the spell
Of a song heard in the distance.
It anchors in your ear,
Like a bugle or a drogue,
And in the atlas you'll find
It comes from Tir-na-nOgue.

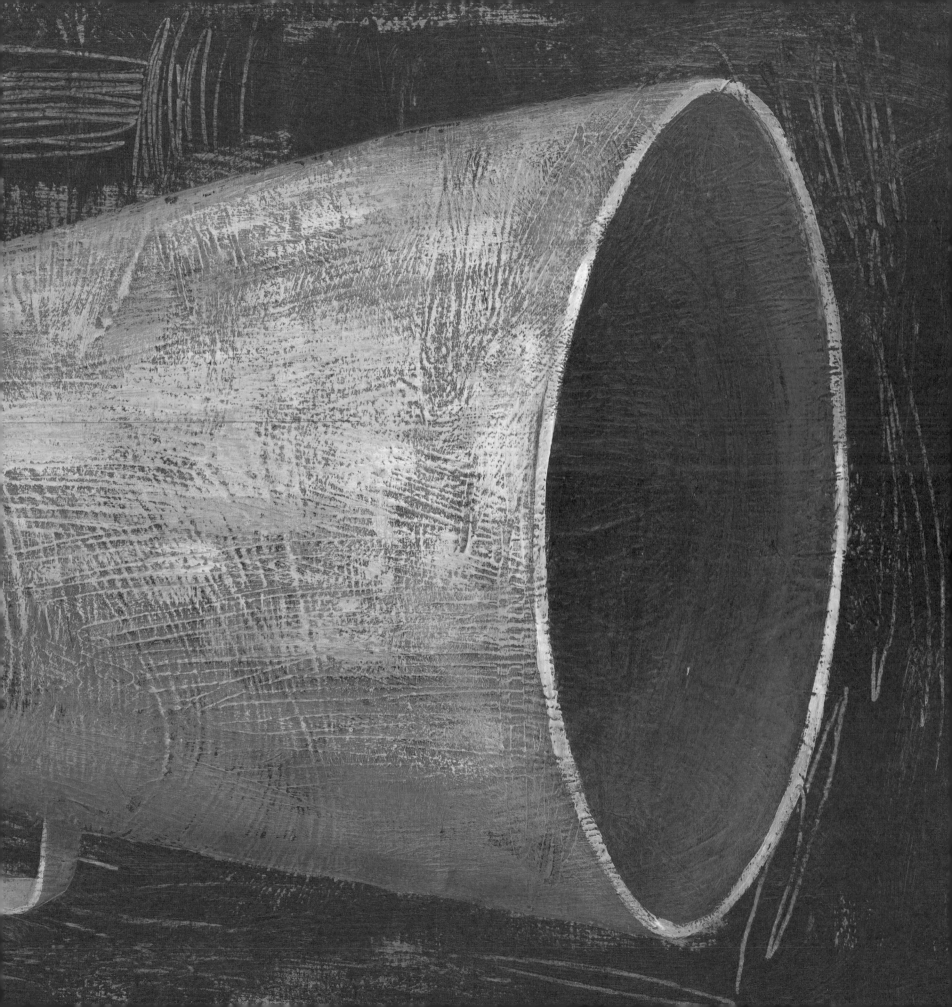

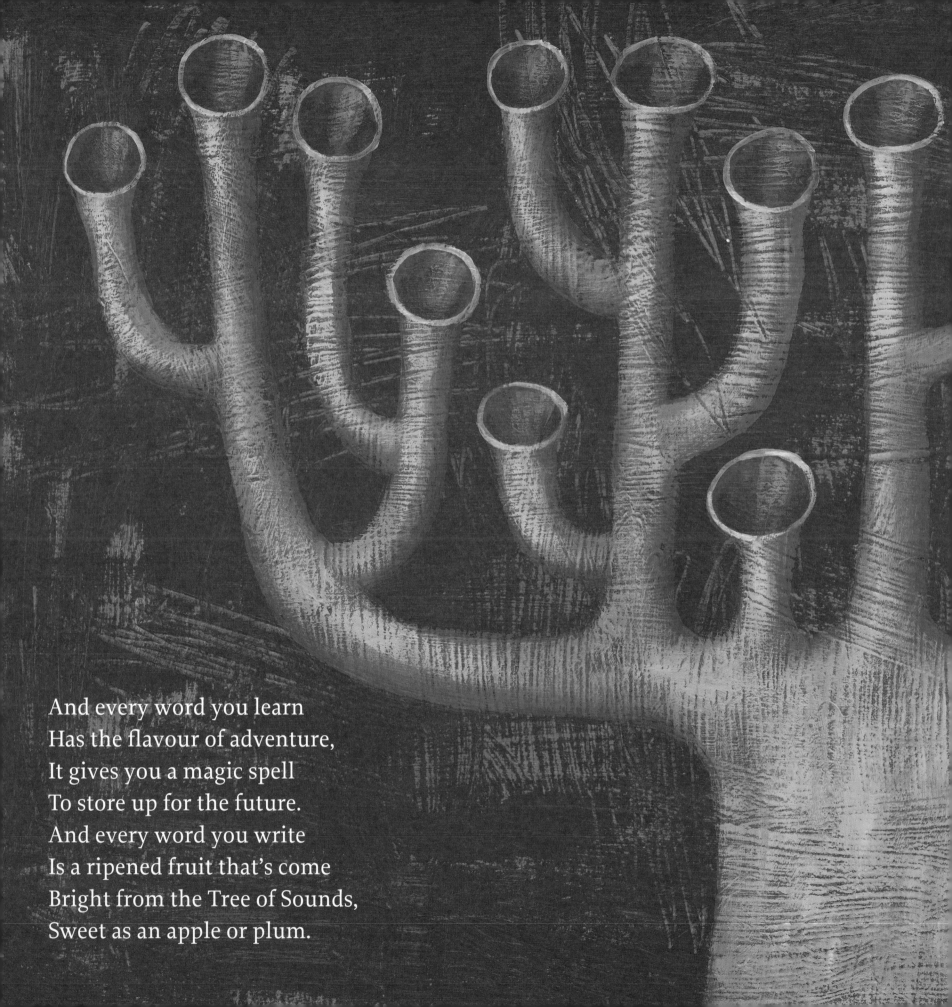

And every word you learn
Has the flavour of adventure,
It gives you a magic spell
To store up for the future.
And every word you write
Is a ripened fruit that's come
Bright from the Tree of Sounds,
Sweet as an apple or plum.

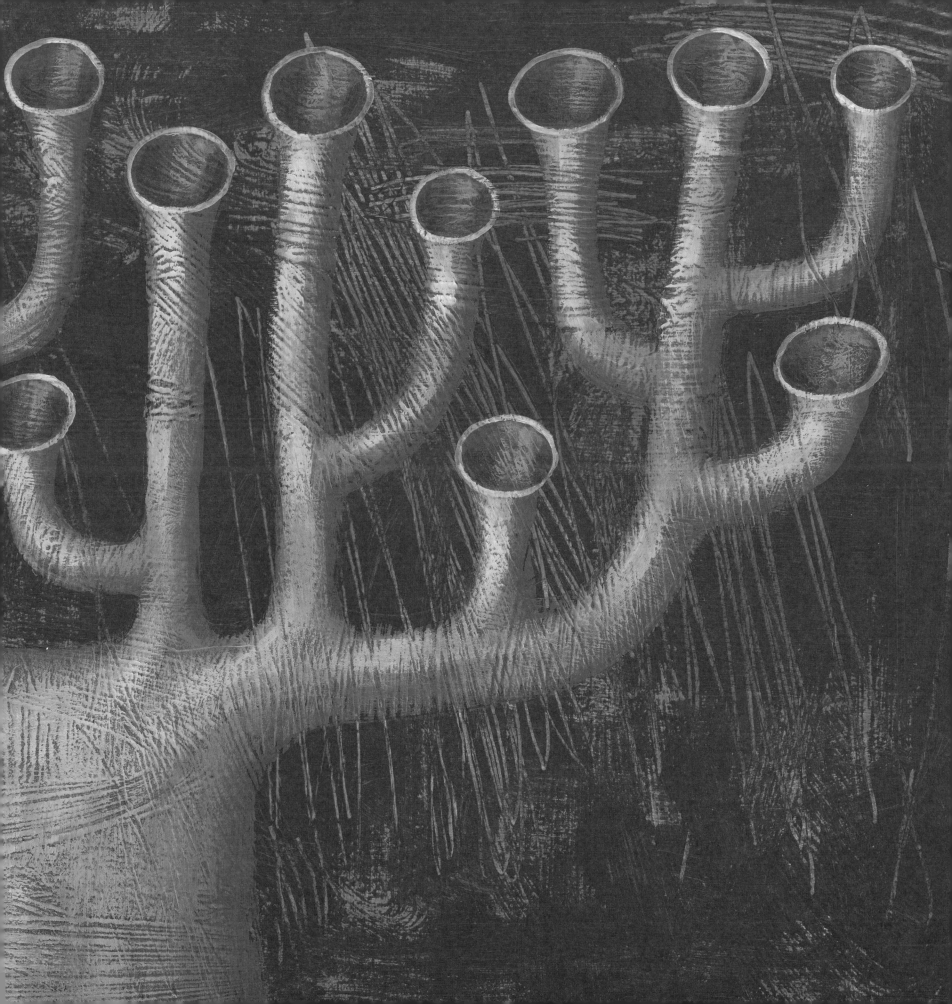

Every word you speak,
And some that make you tremble,
Switches a light bulb on
Inside a darkened window.
Each one swears it has a twin,
A secret it'll share sometime,
Though it'll make your belly ache
If it proves a silly rhyme.

Here we're in a photo,
Taken this Summer past,
Playing on the beach
With things the ocean's cast:
Seaweed, whelks and starfish,
And a spiralling mollusc
Whispering of an island
Where brigands come at dusk.

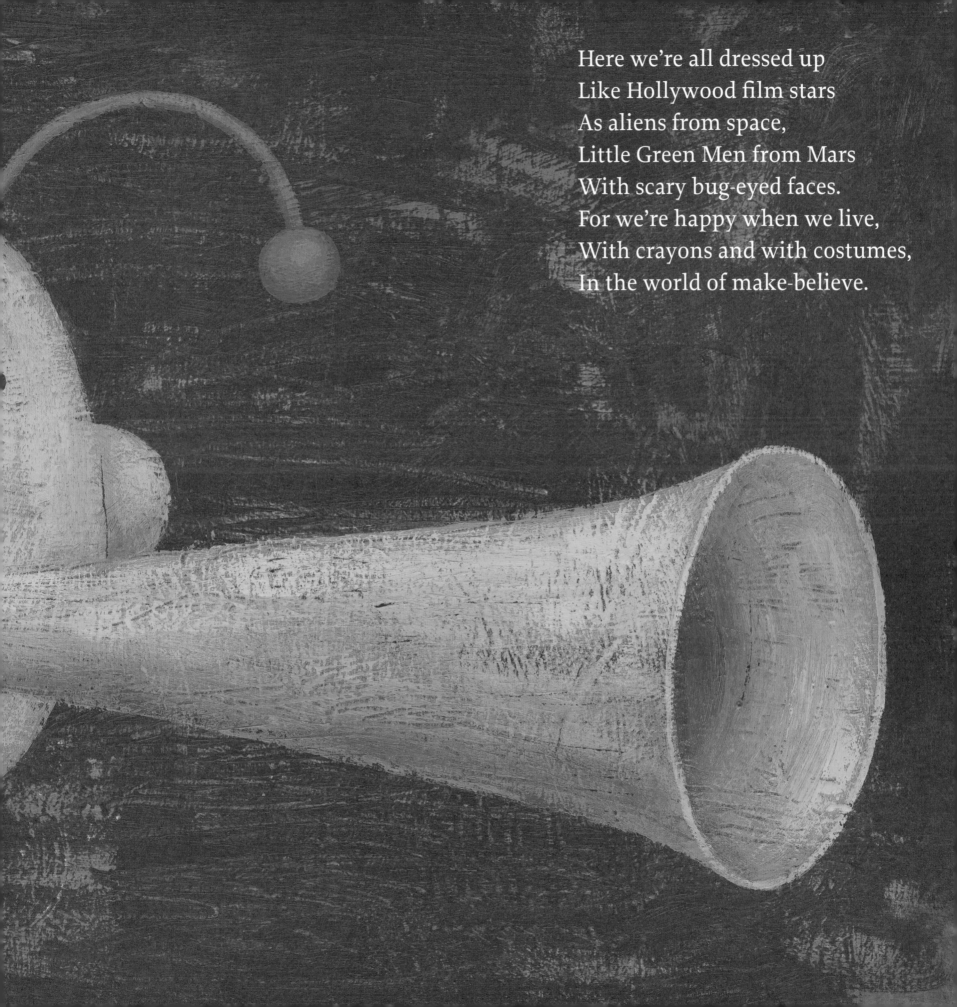

Here we're all dressed up
Like Hollywood film stars
As aliens from space,
Little Green Men from Mars
With scary bug-eyed faces.
For we're happy when we live,
With crayons and with costumes,
In the world of make-believe.

Words somehow flock together
Like swallows on the trees,
Somehow words know each other
Like swarming honey bees.
And somehow words are plusses,
And can't be minus ever,
In the world's addition sum,
Which goes on and on forever.

'Boat!' you shout to the ocean,
'Thirst!' when the sun is hot.
You see the moon in a puddle,
'A wriggly fish I've caught!'
'It's night,' you say, 'I'm sleepy.'
But soon the sky grows grey,
And now light bursts into song
To start another day!

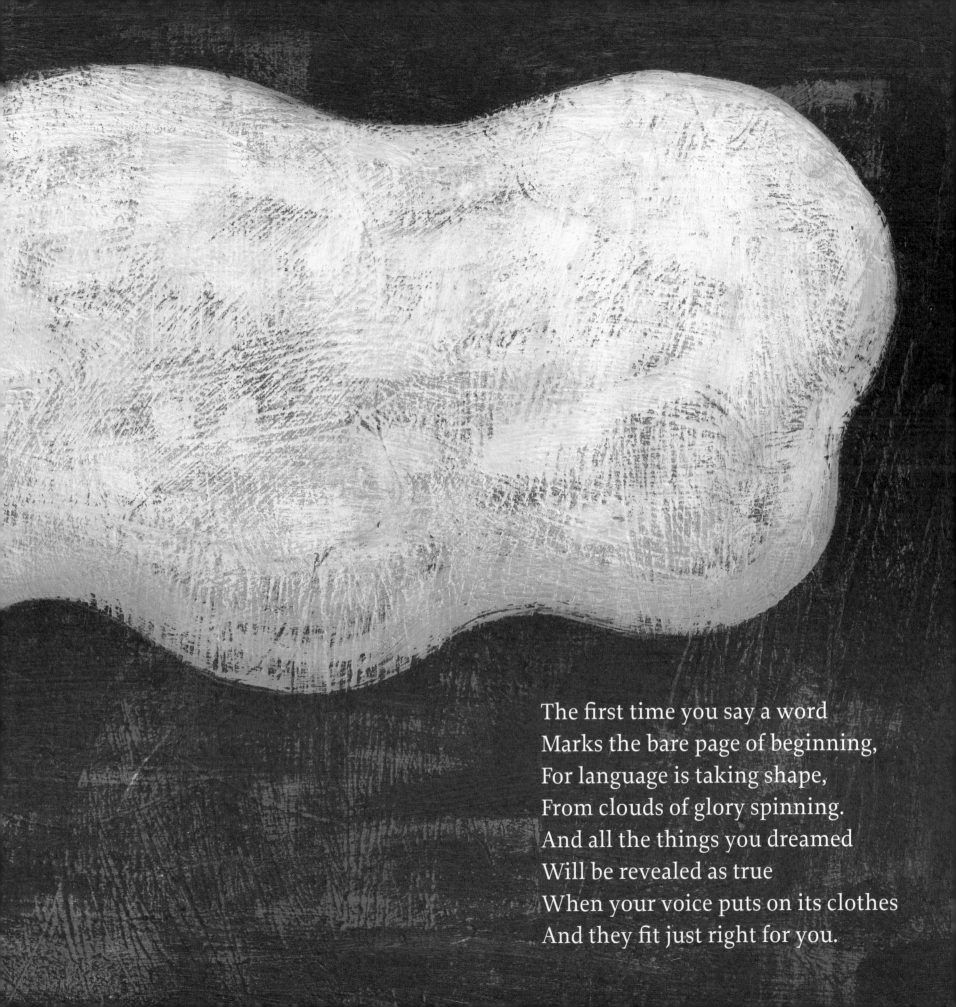

The first time you say a word
Marks the bare page of beginning,
For language is taking shape,
From clouds of glory spinning.
And all the things you dreamed
Will be revealed as true
When your voice puts on its clothes
And they fit just right for you.

And each new word you speak
Reveals some hidden need
Because language is a garden
Which flowers from buried seed.
And all the things you say
Your old folks too once felt,
And our family is an album
Where their memories are kept.

But words can't always tell
The stuff inside your head.
When fingers point and blame
And fill your heart with dread,
You know behind the finger
Some kind intention lies,
But you can't unlock its meaning
Or breach it with your cries.

With a soft ball of yarn
The green cat is playing,
Far away on the farm
The white mare is neighing.
From an old dusty book
You hear a poem shout
Oh, stranger, dear friend,
Read me, please let me out!

Sometimes a rhyme sounds rough,
So odd it puts you off.
But look inside its case,
It's beautiful and soft.
Or some forgotten poet,
Who long since lost his luck,
Whispers his bitter secret
In a rhyme he sweetly struck.

And there are boys at school
Conjuring with the sounds
Until they make believe
They're breaking out of bounds:
With pirates and admirals,
With cutlasses and gore,
Day-dreaming of the world
As it was in days of yore.

Some words belong to Alice,
Who takes them by the hand
And leads them through the Look-
Ing Glass to Wonderland.
There you find their muddy prints
On maps of Topsy-Turvy,
Where books that weigh a ton
Drink stout and sing of Murphy!

But some words you come upon,
In London or Tokyo,
Are such they lead you on
By the nose of Pinocchio.
And when they tell you lies
Then that mischief boy
Teaches the eager reader
That whoppers are a joy.

When words come alive
As pictures in your head,
Lock them in a treasure chest
You put beneath your bed.
There Goldilocks and the bears
Have become best friends,
And Beauty weds the Beast
Before the story ends.

When a boy wakes with a word
Remembered from a dream,
He should write it on his skin,
A tattoo he's brought with him.
It should become the name
Of his true love, or his bear,
Or even the old rag-toy
Which keeps away his fear.

For every word you write
Is writing you as well
And who you are from what you read
Other people tell.
And sometimes on the margins
Of the page a nimble deer,
More beautiful than the words,
Of a sudden will appear.

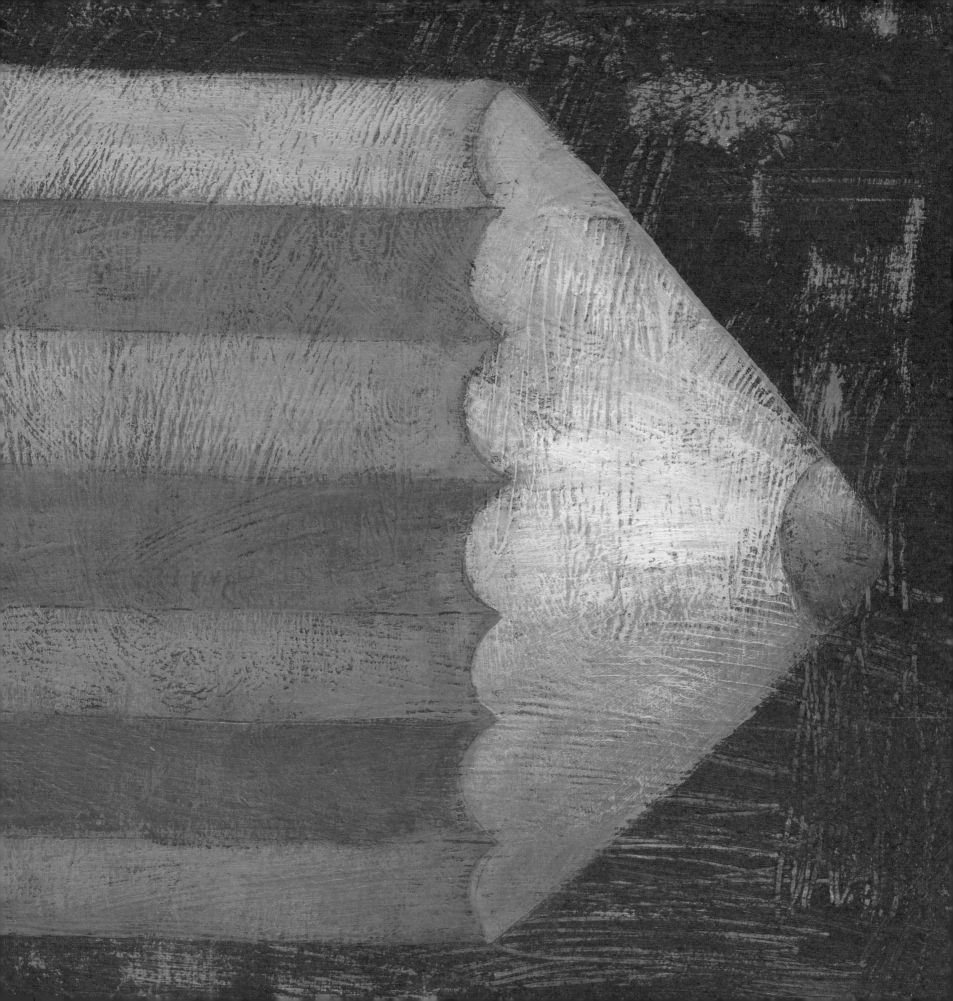

For every word you hear
When you begin to read
Is the first word of a story,
If you give it proper heed.
And every word you add
To those your mind can see
Is one more fairy light
Hung on the Winter Tree.

Sleep-a-bye babies
Safe into the night,
Whose cloak is embedded with jewels,
Its cloth embroidered with light.
Sleep-a-bye babies
Tucked up in your cots,
And send to me your dreams
To bind a black devil with knots.

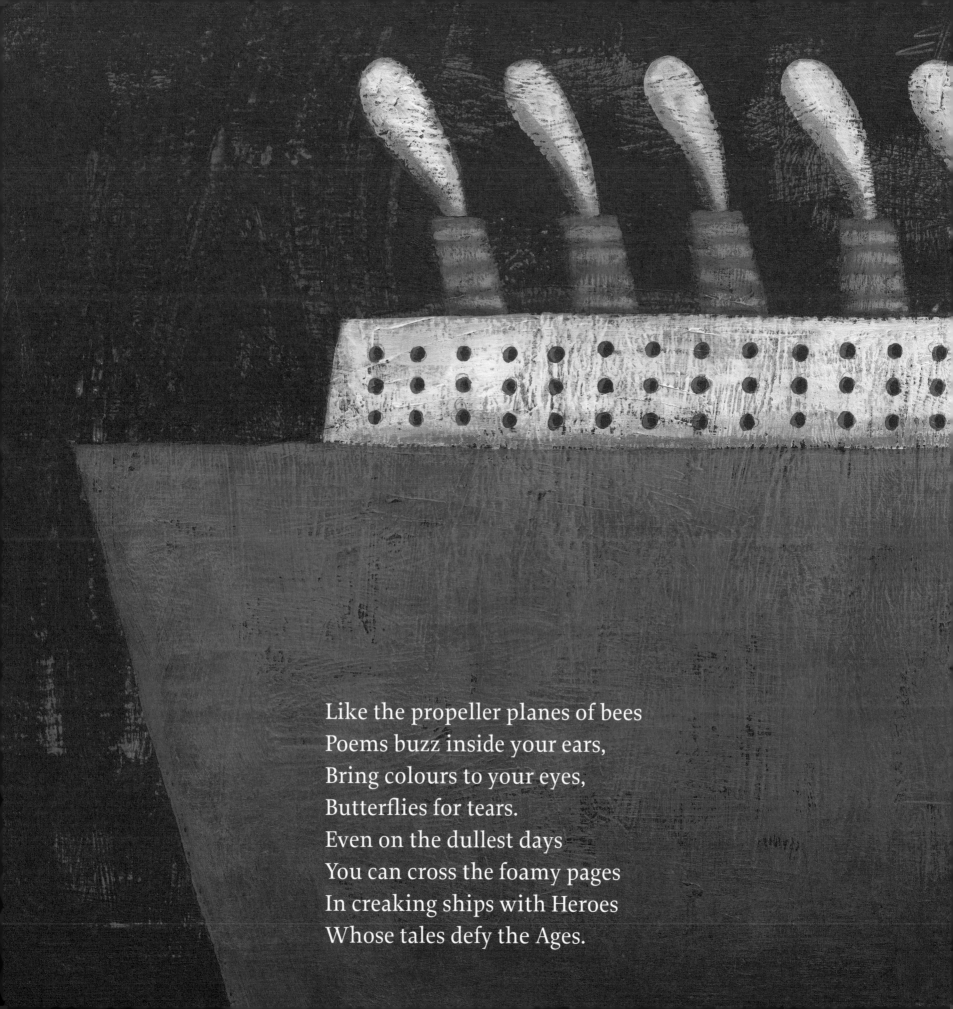

Like the propeller planes of bees
Poems buzz inside your ears,
Bring colours to your eyes,
Butterflies for tears.
Even on the dullest days
You can cross the foamy pages
In creaking ships with Heroes
Whose tales defy the Ages.

These poems which now you know
Is each a treasure trove
Where you can pick 'n choose.
That way you read with love.
In your mind a tree will grow.
So when you dream a word,
Or when new words arrive,
Guard them like the blackbird
Guards its young. Then they thrive.
And when pushed out, when your lungs
Throw them in the air, they live.
They fly and sing melodious.
And that's what Poetry is.